CW00704661

Crow Calls

❧ Volume I ❧

Crow Calls

 Volume I

A COLLABORATIVE ENDEAVOR

EDITED BY
CASSANDRA L. THOMPSON
& MARIE CASEY

QUILL & CROW PUBLISHING HOUSE

CROW CALLS VOLUME ONE. EDITED BY CASSANDRA L. THOMPSON & MARIE CASEY
PUBLISHED BY QUILL & CROW PUBLISHING HOUSE

Copyright © 2021 by Cassandra L. Thompson. Featuring poems by David Andrews, Sophie Brookes, Sara Brunner, Marie Casey, Spyder Collins, Andrew Doughty, Danielle Edwards, Lynn-Cee Faulk, A.L. Garcia, Ayshen Irfan, Ginger Lee, J. Lewis, David Middleham, Erin Quill, Grace Reynolds, Cassandra L. Thompson, Fizzy Twizler, Ravven White, Melanie Whitlock, and K.R. Wieland.

All rights reserved. Published in the United States by Quill & Crow Publishing House, LLC, Ohio. No portion of this book may be reproduced in any form without permission from the publisher, except as permitted by U.S. copyright law.

Designed by Liliana Marie Creative

Printed in the United States of America

ISBN 978-1-7356863-5-6

For the Poetry Community

❧ FEATURING POETRY BY ❧

David Andrews ∽ Sophie Brookes ∽ Sara Brunner
Marie Casey ∽ Spyder Collins ∽ Andrew Doughty
Danielle Edwards ∽ Lynn-Cee Faulk ∽ A.L. Garcia
Ayshen Irfan ∽ Ginger Lee ∽ J. Lewis ∽ David Middleham
Erin Quill ∽ Grace Reynolds ∽ Cassandra L. Thompson
Fizzy Twizler ∽ Ravven White ∽ Melanie Whitlock
and K.R. Wieland

NOTE FROM THE EDITORS

Crow Calls came into fruition as a way to encourage writers to share their poetry on social media, according to certain prompts. Plenty of writers/publishers provide these sorts of prompts, but we wanted to do something different. Horror is often neglected in the literary world, especially after the Halloween buzz dies down, but Quill & Crow Publishing House loves darkly romantic, horrific poetry. We wanted to celebrate macabre themes, even in the month of January. And so, the prompts were created and posted.

What we did not anticipate was the overwhelming response. We quickly realized, after a few days of reading through them, that the poems being shared were absolutely fantastic. We loved watching the prompts evolve in different styles based on the uniqueness of each poet. These were beautiful, heart-felt, and deliciously dark pieces of art. Soon the wheels began turning in owner, Cassandra's, mind and she wondered: what if we published a book of all the different Crow Calls?

Quill & Crow Publishing House is quite pleased to announce that the idea became a reality and is now in your very hands. We are so grateful for all the authors who submitted their poetry to us to create this anthology. It has been an unforgettable experience from start to finish, and we hope to continue the series in the future.

We sincerely hope you will enjoy the unique voices captured in this collection as much as we have.

Dreadfully Yours,

Cassandra L. Thompson & Marie Casey
QUILL & CROW PUBLISHING HOUSE

We walked barefoot,
Dust drifting with each step,
As pebbles dug
Sharp reminders
Of where we stood.
A barren land,
Where perfect faces
Fit in circles,
Only showing slivers of reality.
Until we reached the meadow,
Where the soft grass swayed
Under pale moonlight,
Illuminating our imperfections,
Allowing us to breathe.

❧

DAVID ANDREWS

The curve of your mandible
Rests firmly in the palm of my hand
In a silky kerchief trimmed with black lace
Laden in withered blood red roses
Crushed, just like my depraved beating heart

As the scent wafts in our narrow crypt
My breath turns cold and seeps out whispers
That yearn for death to reunite us once again

I trace my fingertips across our matching coffins

So I lock myself into this familiar tomb,
In my tufted velvet box of royal purple
Punctured by lustrous silver grommets,
To stroke the cheekbone that I used to kiss
"Beloved, it is you that I missed."

∽

BELOVED
GRACE REYNOLDS

Her descent
Crested with starlit iridescence
Little wing
A shudder ripples outward
The dark pool still no more
A silence shattered
By one
Simple
Perfect
Sound
And the heavens wept for their loss
As she fell
With characteristic
Unerring
Grace

David Middleham

Love,
She is a most unforgiving seductress.
Like the mourning dove,

Her majesty visits the restless
Inspiring surreptitiously the need
That renders the most powerful, helpless.

She is a cunning paramour indeed.
Even the gods bow before her grace.
We all proceed

To bare our hearts for her embrace,
And she accepts our tainted offerings
Knowing we have hell to face,

For condemning the bloody, beating things
To her eternal dance amidst infernal rings.

A.L. GARCIA

She had spent a lifetime making herself small,
making herself mouse and fly so that no one noticed her.
Being noticed meant being hit or worse.
So she buried the sunshine, the dandelions, the secret parts of herself.
She didn't bury them inside of her own body.
No, what if a tiger might bubble up and make her sass back
or if a crow laughed or if sadness did a half-ass job on the dishes?
It was safer to keep those things far away from herself.
And so they stayed...
Until the day came when she decided she wanted them back.
Nothing changed, not really, she just thought of how pleasant it would be
to talk, to laugh, to cry without apologizing for it.
To not measure her body everyday to make sure that she wasn't
taking up too much space, too much food, too much existing.
She slipped a powder some kid sold her
into his bottle before the nightly binge began.
She sat, rabbit, gerbil, lizard, making herself as small as possible.
She watched as his eyelids began to close. His chest stopped moving
but his breath was still barely just there. Sparrow, grasshopper, stone.
She took a knife and began to dig into his abdomen. It was messy
and she almost lost her dinner. But finally, she found them.
Just where she had buried them. Dandelions, bubble baths, fireflies, giggles.
Kept safely in his belly, all these years, they were all hers once again.

～

BURIED
LYNN-CEE FAULK

She calls to him
And he sways towards her
Her siren song bewitching
There is no denying her
As he splashes into the water
Swimming towards the maiden
He doesn't notice the others
An entire crew called
Drowned, by the beauty
Of their fantasy come true

୶

K.R. WIELAND

You treat me delicately,
Like a withered rose
With bruised leaves and
Brutally pressed petals -
A fragrance of misery,
Of melancholy, of love.
Of what was and what could be.
And you hold me,
Even as I prick you to match me.
But you say there is beauty in brokenness
And I simply need to be loved
And loved well -
Transformed into a cutting
So I may live again.

❧

MELANCHOLIC ROMANCE
RAVVEN WHITE

My skin falls away
at your barest suggestion
My heart and intestines
slither at your feet
Some people dread
the next phase of obsession
But that's only because
they don't understand
Don't worry, my love
I'll make them...
just for you

∽

ERIN QUILL

barren expanse of sky
no stars dared shine
the night her heart died
even the moon hid
weeping behind a cloud
in utter silent stillness
he carried her lifeless form
clothed in pure white
gently laying her to rest
in the waiting boat
rocking her as though
merely in peaceful slumber
draped in a silk pall
delicately embroidered flowers
her farewell bouquet
with one last kiss pressed
to the soft curve of her lips
he ignited a crimson flame
embarking on a journey
to her final sea grave
and falling to his knees
he wept at the tragic crime
he had committed
the death of her heart
which had only beat for him

༄

DANIELLE EDWARDS

Not all
That has been lost
Is buried
But our love is

And there it shall remain.

ᢙᴥᴐ

MELANIE WHITLOCK

Ravenous
cadaverous
mortuary delight,
my skin embalmed
with his scent,
left throbbing from
necropsy kisses,
vivisection fingers,
and violent trephine lust.

༄

CASSANDRA L. THOMPSON

you ditched me on a beach,
left to chill
frigid air
soiled sand
riddled with needles,
I lay buried in the castles
no skin exposed
too sensitive for rays
yet, you elected departure
knowing good and well
when lightning strikes
I'll mutate to glass
shattering upon your return

∽

MARIE CASEY

You stand, cloaked,
Sheathed in darkness,
Your very essence snuffs out the candles,
I fall to my knees,
Crawling, burrowing, latch myself to you,
Eager to hide in your umbra.

＆

SOPHIE BROOKES

She wore a token hung from a chain
Around her neck a reminder of pain
A tarnished gold key that fit the lock
Keeping her beloved's heart in a box

∽

THE TOKEN
GINGER LEE

Pages of karma fly from my heart
Arrowed words of vulgar acuity

My disassembled existence hunts
That very mockingbird hunter

Voices screech eyes halt in terror
The hunter becomes the hunted

⟡

FIZZY TWIZLER

Broken.
Shattered.
Pieces fall without a sound.
Wracked by misery unspoken,
I clutch your heart to mine
As tears fall on embers scattered,
Your ashes tumble to the ground.

༜

J. LEWIS

Mourning moments
Like only lovers can
Bare skin and the chill of stone
An epitaph carved deeper
A notion of desire
To embalm
Upon a haunted grace
Preservation of something sweeter
Than the rose scent of your tomb

❧

DAVID MIDDLEHAM

In the pale glow of an empty restaurant,
Candle flames flicker in the shifting currents
Of your aquamarine eyes.

Departing -
To the decaying brick of city streets
Fingers tentatively find relief in empathetic hands
Threatening vibrations curse the night -
In a call from reality,
Gutting the moment -
Suggesting an unavoidable end to this dream.

Yet the rain would fall,
Washing away the fallacy
That we are prisoners to our circumstances,
That we must settle for what we no longer desire.

༄

DAVID ANDREWS

She roasted his heart on a spitfire
To cremate the remains of love
Then threw her own into the pyre
So it might all be done at once
But it refused to burn
Blackened on the edges
It was returned to her
Mangling the solemn pledge
To never feel again
Ashes smoldering in vain

❧

A.L. GARCIA

you wanted to see inside
so, I grabbed the tools,
shovels and smiles
I cleared the pall of black smoke
with hopeful thoughts
and painful reminders
but once clothes hit the floor
the digging stopped
and it reinforced the all barriers

⁓

MARIE CASEY

Beloved
Remember when I was yours?
Me neither
Another wasted wish
Upon a burning star.

❦

MELANIE WHITLOCK

That pretty delicate thing
Myself, I couldn't contain
But after the first taste
Left with loathsome disdain
Her poison infused
Under the skin
One drop of blood between lips
And I writhed within

⁓

ONE DROP
GINGER LEE

As Death's icy hands envelope me
These staring eyes no longer see;
Her rictus hands in silence plea,
She thought a tortured soul to free.

She dressed as when we first married,
Though none knew the pain she carried;
Shunned, scorned night and day unvaried,
Countless times the knife she buried.

Innocence, purity now lost-
She sees, she knows the line was crossed;
A heart so pure now turned to frost,
My life was not too dear a cost.

J. LEWIS

The weeping willow
Whose bark remembers
A first kiss and lovers names
Carved into a heart on her skin
Stretches out her arms, now barren of leaves,
Each one a distant memory.

If she could bring back
The warmth of summer and skipped heartbeats
It would carry her through the winter,
Whose bitterness, her bark remembers.

∽

BITTER
GRACE REYNOLDS

Leeches suckle
blood curdling poison
out of my veins,
my mind lost to arsenic dreams
and laudanum lullabies,
my final breaths laced
with belladonna
and the aroma of a love lost
but still lingering in the cockles
of my decaying heart.

∽

CASSANDRA L. THOMPSON

horrid creature caressed her chin
with one wretched claw
touch as cold as winter's chill
spindly finger digging deeper
drawing forth ruby beads
adornment 'round her throat
wide innocent eyes flashed
with a hint of defiant spark
staring in spite of the flinch of pain
"I will have your heart of gold"
rasped in a cruel tone
"but I am fond of cat and mouse games
so I shall set you free
flee where you might child
but you shall not escape from me"
wild she crashed through bramble and brush
thorns tearing at her pale flesh
under moonlight's haunting shadows
casting furtive glances back upon her stumbled path
owl's bloodcurdling screech
pierced through the silence of the woods
a warning sign of evil at hand
with no place to run and hide
whispers and mocking laughs
assaulted her tender ears
tossing her whirling mind into
a disorienting gyration
her heart pounding within her chest
drumming beckoning sealing her foretold fate
one gasp - she never had a chance
in a instant, the blink of an eye
she lay in a growing pool of blood
sudden victim of the night

❧

DANIELLE EDWARDS

Rouge-stained cheeks; smeared crimson lips
From a shattered nose, Stygian blood drips
Cracking flesh of fragile porcelain
Sickly-sweet perfume; miasma of sin
Pure-black eyes stare haunted, aghast
At the Doll Maker and his uniform cast
Endless boys and girls are birthed
Embattling an army of the accursed
No mere mortal can resist their wit or charm
The broken children wielding guile to disarm
Only once you've welcomed them into your home
Can you hear the true shrill of their wretched tone?
By then—oh, no! —it is too late
The Doll Maker has sealed your fate
All those miniature boys and girls
With dead eyes and angelic curls
Upon you they shall descend
Another doll in the army of the condemned

ᐰ

DOLL MAKER'S CURSE
AYSHEN IRFAN

This pain bites at me
It burns
Twists my insides
Beats me down
Walks me
To places I haven't been
In such a long time.
Wish I'd die
Memories keep me
But I don't need to be
Still, this pain it weaves
Through my soul
I shudder to think
How much worse
It could be
This pain
It taunts me and toys
Running through me
Like a riptide
A sneaker wave
Pulling me out to sea.
Pain is so lonely.

✺

SPYDER COLLINS

In a dreamlike blur
I am lost
Within the moss and the crumbled decay
The wildwood,
In its terrifying majesty,
Has consumed me
I am to be slowly digested
By rough lichens and smooth fungi
Slime moulds and tentacles of roots
The air here is ancient
Full of spores and diatoms
The bronchia become branches
I am choked and composted
Marrow becomes loam
Bones become wood
A pall of leaves covers my outline
And I am forgotten

WILDWOOD
ANDREW DOUGHTY

an empty cup
barren cascades,
no drip drip
or drop drop,
not even dribbles
to feast on
only dubious echos
blaring reruns
in your ear
yammering and yammering
pretending to flow
but please remember,
water soothes
and an empty cup
coos recycled lies.

⁓

MARIE CASEY

They say we live in shadows -
An umbra of mystery -
But we are far more transparent
Than what we're claimed to be.
You're told that we're kept hidden
And only show up here and there,
That you'll know us by the burning sun,
Twinkling skin, or silken hair.
But really, dear, the difference
You'd probably seldom see -
Unless you feel for heartbeats
Or graze our pointed teeth.

∽

VAMPIRIC UMBRA
RAVVEN WHITE

Lush
Green
Dotted with
Sunflowers
Roses
Lilacs
And lilies
Beckoning
Life
Love
Joy

Only a memory

Humans
A plague
Destroyers
Of all
Leave
A barren
Decayed
And rotten
Grief
Where beauty
Once lived

❧

ERIN QUILL

I lay them down,
Dead lilies,
At your porcelain feet,
A gift of mercy,
For you,
Goddess of Infertility,
The Barren Mother.

༄

SOPHIE BROOKES

In the world's eye
Sands of time are dusty

Futures unseen buried to the naked eye
Only I can make my future clear
Only I can look to the sky

See what he has given me
To dig out of this golden muck

But devils and demons...hold my ankles tight

❧

Fizzy Twizler

I sleep to escape the torment of day
Close my eyes, embracing amnesia
Melatonin, nature's anaesthesia
Colours of the late dusk fading to grey
Oh, such frightful dreams!
Crows blinding me with cutlasses of bone
Clawed feet clench, throttling my bloodied throat
Horned shadow beast, the devil's goat
Angelic wings wide, atop a soulless throne
Oh, awaken me!

༚

NIGHTMARES
AYSHEN IRFAN

I woke from a surreal dream.
Everything in place, so it would seem.
Crimson rose from me like steam.
Led me to believe I was still in a dream.

I see me, the wraith I've become.
Hideous, soul-eater, and loathsome.
Indeed life is a chore, cumbersome.
But I move on, despite what I've become.

So tomorrow will become a new day.
A chance for a wraith to hide away.
Is there a reason for me to stay?
Seems I am here for one more day.

༄

SPYDER COLLINS

Cut you open to the core, hear the bones crack
Spilt you right to the marrow
Watch as my eyes turn pitch black
And your capillaries start to narrow
Your life begins to flashback
This is like music to my ears, a concerto
What now, you are the one having a panic attack?
Before I am done with you, my soul with turn to absolute zero
This will make me climax
It's not like I can be any clearer
Your life comes to a close as I begin to hack
So go on and shove me in this oesophagus,
I will rise like the scarab, six feet below
I'll break the Pharaoh's golden stack
And once I'm done
you will be the marionette in my puppet show
While your desecrated soul,
Osiris wouldn't even take back.

∽

SARA BRUNNER

Come sit with me,
my old melancholy,
my dearest friend,
we'll hold hands
and watch the birds go by
just as we used to do,
so many nights, so many nights ago.

I might have appeared alone all those times,
to the happily uninitiated,
but you were all always right there for me:

night and stars and the ability to disappear,
the little creek was there and the big creek too.
An enormous tree, indestructible and sleepy.
My protectors, and you, watching over me.
to shield me from things even worse than a wistful nostalgia.

⁓

MELANCHOLY
LYNN-CEE FAULK

Winter Child of Sorrows
stands in her snow globe of ashes,
lodged between mossy warrior skulls
and crumbling castle ruins.
She knows her misery is of her own making,
yet she still longs for love and sunlight,
though she knows,
for her,
they do not exist.

༄

CASSANDRA L. THOMPSON

I sat, covered in dirt
singing to a melancholy sky
the stars, I crave your shine
your burning fires
infernos of celestial life
but not tonight
no, your light is dim
and it makes me weep
knowing your fires
are as extinguishable as mine

∽

MARIE CASEY

Who will shed a tear when they close my coffin
When my face is seen for the very last time
How long before I'm completely forgotten
After the death bell rings its final chime
And the pall has fallen
Blown away from the wind, and disappearing into the Rhine
My body becoming food for the flowers to feed the pollen
The harsh winter turning to Springtime
Because in the end I was just so common
Nothing sublime
Just a worn out soul past her prime
And now as I'm rotting
And my body has softened
I realize there is no divine
Just more darkness in this confine

Sara Brunner

Piano keys of dark ivy leaves
Played by the rods of rain
Gravestones glisten slightly brighter
Than the low Heron grey sky
A bleak and broken landscape
A cold and lonely place
The deepest well,
A sump filled with melancholy
Drawn and lifted
To flow across every surface
Gather every tear
Draining back down
Through the airless bones

⁓

HERON GREY SKY
ANDREW DOUGHTY

Autolysis
Putrefaction
Bloat
Active decay
Advance decay

I have passed my living days
My ash flutters about a wisp
As my soul has been led astray
And now I fade to the mist

Blood-curdling cries rain down
From angels who cast shadows
Across tainted and unholy ground
Where the sinful and forsaken go

Listen and you can hear
The cry of my forgotten soul
As a descend to a place of fear
To the sound of the bells final toll

❧

SPYDER COLLINS

They said that she was worthless
Used up, a hopeless case
And she believed the lies
That she was broken
Until one day she saw something
Something new within herself
And she became more
Than what she was before
Defying all their words
Turning the past
And the pain
And the memories
To ash

K.R. WIELAND

AUTHOR BIOGRAPHIES

DAVID ANDREWS is an accidental poet who spends his lunch breaks pondering the world so he can create poems by nightfall. An avid sports fan, when he is not writing, he enjoys running and spending time with his family and dogs. This is his first publication.

As of yet, unpublished, and hoping to break into freelance writing, SOPHIE BROOKES is passionate about Gothic and LGBTQIA+ fiction. An avid reader of both Poe and Wilde in her teens is most likely the culprit there! She is currently working on a coming-of-age visual novel and a Tolkien inspired poetry collection, both of which she hopes to complete at some point during her lifetime. When she is not writing, Sophie loves gaming and cosplaying.

SARA BRUNNER lives in Lakewood, New York, with her nana, who she takes care of. She started writing dark poetry in October and got back into graphic art after a dear friend's encouragement. This is her first publication.

MARIE CASEY is a writer and a mysterious presence. In her past life, she was a timid, cave-dwelling mouse. Now she seeks to experience the sunlight in the dream of sharing her thoughts, feelings, and words with the flowers she has admired for years.

A man of many faces, SPYDER COLLINS haunts the caves of Colorado, where he weaves disturbing tales of horror and suffering. When he is not agitating the minds of unsuspecting readers, he pens soul-shattering poetry. Sometimes he does both. His work was featured in the anthology, *Twisted Love*, and has recently released a poetry collection called *Adrift on a Sea of Shadows*.

ANDREW DOUGHTY is a 42-year-old poet, photographer, and nature writer. He is a cemetery keeper and woodsman as his day job in Lincolnshire, UK. His poetry reflects his emotions surrounding the oldest subjects: love, death, and nature.

As a child, DANIELLE EDWARDS could often be found curled up devouring books for hours on end. Now with two sweet, energetic boys of her own, her special kiddos at her physical therapy job, and a few friendly felines, she finds herself devoting less time to reading, and more to spilling her heart out on the page. When she isn't writing her story, she enjoys spending time with family, friends, nature, and the arts.

LYNN-CEE FAULK has been obsessed with reading and writing for as long as they could read and write. Reading supplied a window to the world outside of their small farming community in South Georgia and a roadmap to a way of being other than what their disordered upbringing provided. They still believe in the power of the written word to change lives. As a writer, poetry was their first love and they have published two chapbooks: *Confessions: Micropoetry on Love, Loss, and Longing* and *A Pound of Pale Winter Blues*.

A.L. GARCIA lives in Massachusetts with her loving husband and two spirited children. She spends her days reveling in the chaos of her babes, writing, reading, and balancing other obligations, as many mothers do. She began writing poetry as a youth as a way of coping with abusive family dynamics. She joined the writing community in August of 2020, after independently publishing a personal narrative detailing the abuse she endured as a child. Her first poetry collection is set to be released later this year. She is a veteran of the U.S. Army and studied Sociology and Social Science at Towson University.

AYSHEN IRFAN is a born-and-bred Brightonian with a passion for dark and urban fantasy, both of which she writes. She first established her predilection for the occult and arcane as a young girl, and her particular penchant for vampires is evident within her tales. As a practising Witch, Ayshen incorporated some of her under-standing—especially in regards to intent and energy magick—into her work, which is displayed in her debut novel, book one in the *Scarlet Cherie: Vampire Series, The Fire Within My Heart.*

GINGER LEE is a Tennessee born poet and 2020 NYC Big Book Award Distinguished Favorite winning indie author of everything romance. Member of Dark Poets Club and collector of music, art, and Monster High Dolls. Coffee and taco fanatic.

Born before "Video Killed the Radio Star" aired on MTV, J. LEWIS has always been an avid reader. His favorite works include *Les Miserables* by Victor Hugo, *The Wheel of Time* series by Robert Jordan, and everything written by Edgar Allen Poe. He is currently writing a historical fiction romance set during the American Civil War. The poems included in this anthology are his first published works.

DAVID MIDDLEHAM is from Birmingham where he is mostly found wearing headphones or watching terrible movies. He writes poetry, literary fiction and has so far self-published a book of love poems.

ERIN QUILL loves writing poetry that both strikes at the mind and captures the heart. She began her poetry journey at the age of five when she penned her first haiku. Ms. Quill has been published twice. Once under the title, "Flirting with Vikings" in the *Of Cottages and Cauldrons* anthology. And a second time under her "erinquill8" Twitter handle in the *Crispy Rooftop Conversation Stories*, edited by Scott Christopher Beebe.

GRACE REYNOLDS writes about the dark and obscure fantasies of life. Her writing invites readers to look at the everyday things around them to wonder what gruesome scenario they will find themselves in next. When she is not writing, she is reading or attending to the daily responsibilities of a domestic engineer.

Horror writer and part-time dark goddess, CASSANDRA L. THOMPSON has been creating stories since she got her grubby little hands around a pen. When she is not busy managing a house full of feral children (human and canine), you can find her wandering around cemeteries, taking pictures of abandoned things, or in the library doing research. She is the founder of Quill & Crow Publishing House, the author of *The Ancient Ones Trilogy*, and scribe for Hekate for In the Pantheon. But mostly, she is staring off into space, imaging other worlds and things that go bump in the night.

FIZZY TWIZLER is a 47-year-old helpdesk advisor from London with a keen interest in Archeology and Egyptology. Her poetry and micro-fiction has been published in various online magazines and she has published anthologies available on Amazon. She also had a poem read aloud by Deelite Radio for Christmas, 2020.

RAVVEN WHITE is a gothic poet specializing in themes of love, grief, and growth, and her beloved darklings. Ravven will soon be publishing her own collections of dark poetry and gothic novels. She lives in a castle by the sea with her husband, daughter, and two hell hounds.

MELANIE WHITLOCK is a writer, historian, and poet hailing from Cumbria. With supernatural roots from her grandparents, her life is rich with magic and steeped in folklore. Her writing work has been included in national magazines and newspapers, and she uploads short pieces daily to Twitter. Her first supernatural/romance novel is expected late next year. You can find her between the moon and stars.

K. R. WIELAND has always had an over abundant love of creating. Whether it is with a paintbrush, a pen or typing away at her computer, she is always trying to make something. When she is not writing or painting, she can be found at home dancing in the kitchen with her daughters or talking about all things nerdy or foodie with her husband.

Discover more at
www.quillandcrowpublishinghouse.com

Printed in Great Britain
by Amazon

67606595R00038